Other People's Fu**ing

An Oxford Affair

A.L. Rowse & Adam Von Trott

By

David Slattery-Christy

DEDICATION

For Oxford. The city of my birth and place that will always
be my spiritual home

My admiration for Adam von Trott and the tenacity, courage and
fearlessness he demonstrated in his opposition to Hitler and the disaster he
wrought on Germany. The world could do with many more men like him.
Alfred Leslie Rowse for being stubborn, difficult and unafraid to voice his
opinions about what he saw as the disastrous 20th century. Through writing
this play I got to know and admire them in equal measure.

Last but not least for my father Leslie John Slattery who knew
Alfred Leslie Rowse whilst they were at All Souls College, Oxford, during
the 1950s and 1960s. Rowse as a Fellow and historian, my father as a butler
and wine connoisseur. Their common bond and friendship was a dream of
a better world for everyone.

A CIP Catalogue record for this book is available from the British Library, London.

Published by Christyplays

www.christyplays.com

@DSCAuthor

With Thanks

A.L. Rowse for the inspiration to write this play.

Oliver Mahoney, Archivist, Lady Margaret Hall, Oxford.

Anna Sander, Archivist & Curator of Manuscripts, Balliol College, Oxford.

Christopher White, OUDS President, Magdalen College, Oxford.

Professor Sir John Vickers, Warden, All Souls College, Oxford.

Michael Harvey; Raymond Langford Jones; Graham Greenwood and my Agent Robert Smith Literary Agency, London.

Further Reading

Ollard, Richard. A Man of Contradictions, A Life of A.L. Rowse. *Allen Lane, Penguin Press, London. 1999.*

Sears, Kenneth A.E. Opposing Hitler, Adam von Trott zu Solz. *Sussex Academic Press, Brighton, United Kingdom. 2009*

Ollard, Richard. The Diaries of A.L. Rowse [edited]. *Allen Lane, Penguin Books, London. 2003.*

Hopkinson, Diana. The Incense Tree. *Routledge & Kegan Paul Limited, London. 1968*

Rowse, A.L. Homosexuals in History. *Dorset Press, Marboro Books Corp. United Kingdom. 1983.*

NOTES ON INCLUSIONS

I wanted to include the early recordings of Al Bowlly from 1929 to the 1930s simply because they are so evocative of that era. Bowlly's recordings are in the Public Domain [https://archive.org/details/AlBowllyPart4/] so a PRS licence would be required. My idea is that the actor who plays Al Bowlly will mime to these original recordings included in the play.

If I Had You (Ted Campbell Shapiro / EMI Music Pub.)
Close Your Eyes (Mike De Scala / Universal Music Pub.)
The Very Thought of You (Ray Noble/Al Bowlly /Campbell, Connelly & Co.)
Blue Moon (Richard Rodgers / R&H Music)
With My Eyes Wide Open (Harry Revel/Mack Gordon)
Remember Me (Robert Millar)
Night and Day (Cole Porter /Warner/Chappell Music Ltd.)

I also included interwoven in the dialogue are some of Rowse's own diary entries relating to his relationship with Adam von Trott and Oxford. A Shakespeare sonnet and soliloquy, Chamberlain's War Declaration and a quote from Hitler's Mein Kampf. Also Rowse's poem dedicated to Adam.

[1] Rowse's diary entry. Pg. 9 ; [2] Venice quote attributed to David Cecil. Pg. 10 ;
[3] Shakespeare sonnet 104 Pg. 12 [4] Rowse's diary entry Pg. 33 ;
[5] Mein Kampf by A. Hitler Pg.43; [6] Hamlet Soliloquy Shakespeare. Pg82;
[7] Chamberlain War Broadcast Pg.86 [8] Rowse quote Pg.91[9]Rowse quote Pg.92;
[10] Rowse's poem to Adam Pg. 92.

Act One

Scene 1: All Souls Quad. 1929. Early evening. Michaelmas Term.

Scene 2: All Souls Quad. Later that night.

Scene 3: Rowse's Rooms. All Souls. Next Morning.

Scene 4: Rowse's Rooms. All Souls. A few weeks later.

Scene 5: Rowse's Rooms. All Souls. 1931. Afternoon. Trinity Term.

Scene 6: Adam von Trotts study. Germany 1931.

Act Two

Scene 1: Election Count – Cornwall. 1931.

Scene 2: Bodleian Quad. 1931. Early evening. Michaelmas Term.

Scene 3: Rowse's Rooms. All Souls. 1933. Hilary Term.

Scene 4: Rowse's Rooms. All Souls – Later.

Scene 5: Adam's Dream and Dance Sequence.

Scene 6: Rowse's Rooms. All Souls. 1938. Early hours.

Scene 7: Chamberlain's Speech/ Hitler Broadcast.

Scene 8: Rowse's Rooms. All Souls. 1944. Trinity Term.

A.L. Rowse at All Souls College, Oxford, at the time my
my father knew him in the 1950s.

Characters

Alfred Leslie Rowse – Academic & Don [age 27+]
Adam von Trott zu Solz – German Baron [age 20+]
Jackers – All Souls College Porter [age 40+]
Vickers – All Souls Chapel Curate [age 28+]
Lady Price – Veronica's Mother [age 50s]
Veronica Price – Student & Friend [age 20+]
Diana Hubb – Student & Friend [age 20+]
Al Bowlly – 1930s singer [age 31+]

Voice Over Characters:

BBC Radio News Presenter (Male) – 1930s
BBC Radio Presenter (Female) of the
Light Programme – 1930s

Adam von Trott zu Solz during his time at
Oxford in the 1930s

Note from Playwright

The more I discovered about A.L Rowse and Adam von Trott the more I was intrigued. It struck me that they had an odd kind of bond that seemed to rise above sexuality or the normal kind of boundaries expected in everyday relationships. They said themselves that somehow their "souls" had connected. This I believe is what became the enduring and everlasting bond between them. Rowse died many years after Adam but still he held that love for him in his heart – indeed so did many others who fell in love with Adam during his time at Oxford. And there were many, including Diana Hubbuck who I have loosely based the character of Diana on in this play. The character of Veronica is also loosely based on Veronica Wedgwood – later Dame C.V. Wedgwood. The characters of Jackers the porter, and Vickers the curate, are purely of my imagination. The play can only ever be my interpretation of what happened. That said it has been informed by letters, diaries and books the main protagonists left behind for posterity. I feel I know them all after writing this play; and certainly have an affection for them because of it.

My father's friendship with Rowse during the 1950s and 1960s is encouraging. Mostly because as Rowse himself said many times that he considered most people third or fourth-rate and not worth speaking to at all. That my father became someone worthy of being a friend, who spent holidays at his Cornwall home, speaks volumes. Sometimes I feel that Rowse was actually very insecure. He made outrageous statements, and railed against the snobbery he experienced at Oxford by some, to shock them and the world of academia. In spite of his brilliance, he never felt he fitted in. My father had academic aspirations but had not had the opportunities to fulfill them because of WW2. Perhaps this was the foundation of their friendship?

David Slattery-Christy - 2017

A young Rowse at Oxford (centre) with friends Roger Makins and Evelyn Baring. Photographed in 1926 by Lady Ottoline Morrelll

Other People's Fu**ing!

ACT ONE

Scene 1:

Michelmas term.1929

Saturday evening in the quad of All Souls College. Light shines from inside the Codrington library illuminating the stained glass windows. The college clock chimes the half hour – it is 7.30pm. Other chimes in the distance echo eerily.

Jackers the college porter enters and crosses to a young man sitting on a bench – he is dressed for a formal dinner in white tie and tails. He smokes nervously. Jackers removes his bowler hat before he speaks to him.

Jackers

Herr Trott?

Adam

Yes?

Jackers

Professor Selbie has asked me to find you. He would like you
to join them for drinks prior to dinner.
Shall I escort you through, sir?

Adam

No. No, thank you. I am waiting for…

Jackers

Mr. Rowse? I did mention to you that he had left the college earlier and he did not leave word when he would return, sir. They serve dinner exactly at eight, sir. You wouldn't want to be late.

Adam

I understand. Thank you for your kindness, but I shall…

Rowse appears and is rushing. He crosses towards the stone stairs that lead to his rooms and starts to climb them. Adam rushes over and shouts him. As this happens Jackers shakes his head, puts his bowler hat back on, and exits.

Rowse! Is it you?

Adam is standing at the foot of the stairs looking up at Rowse. Rowse peers down at him and seems transfixed at the sight of him. He studies his eyes.

Rowse

Herr Trott? You remembered my name. I didn't expect
to see you again so soon – you
said you would not come to dinner.

Adam

Please, call me Adam. I know, I changed my mind. My aunt Beatrix
sent me the money to by a suitable dinner suit. Used.
Will it do?

Rowse

Perfectly. You go in! I will go and dress for dinner and join you
shortly. Go! Tell Professor Selbie I will be there.

Rowse disappears up the stairs. Adam watches as he goes. He then turns and exits towards the dining hall.

Scene 2:

As the lights fade we hear the Al Bowlly recording of
IF I HAD YOU *This aids the scene change.*

We see Al Bowlly singing into a microphone.

If I Had You

Song ends - The lights fade out on Al Bowlly..

Later that night: Jackers appears holding up a lantern – he is returning to the lodge after his night patrol. After he has passed Adam and Rowse emerge into the quad. The music ends.
They are laughing and have had a good evening together.
Rowse helps Adam as he is jovial after a little too much champagne and wine.
They sit on a bench.

Rowse

Quiet, Adam. Jackers will hear us and then
there will be trouble. You can call me Leslie if you like.

Adam

It's like being at school with Jackers – you are a grown Fellow.
No, I prefer to call you Rowse. It makes me
laugh – it sounds like an angry little dog. Rowse!

Rowse

Charming, I'm sure. (*he laughs*) The college porters are like god.
Upset them at your peril. So, does Adam have an Eve?

Adam

No. Adam has lots of people who admire him,
or desire him, for his looks but not his intellect. There is no depth

to their interest in him. People can be idiots and obsessed with the mere superficialities, can't they?

Rowse

Indeed! Do you know, you are the first man I have ever talked to who makes me feel comfortable – no, you make me feel equal. I don't feel I have to prove myself to you.
How very odd.

Adam

Equal to whom? My title of Baron makes me a mere breeding machine to some. You discuss things with me, even trivial ordinary things, that has respect for my place as a fellow person in this awful world.

Rowse

What is your place? Do any of us really have one? I am not sure I know what mine is although I would like to make a difference, change things for the better somehow. You may be an aristocrat, but you don't have the arrogance of some. Just cynicism for the world!

Adam

My heart belongs to Germany – but my soul, for some reason I cannot explain, will always belong here - if that is possible in such a short time. One day, Rowse my friend, I intend to join you here as a Fellow at All Souls.

Rowse

Oxford has the habit of taking one's soul captive and never letting it go. It's a blessing and a curse. (*he relays it as he sees it in his mind's eye*) [1] 'I still remember my first excitement on coming back to Christ Church as an undergraduate, entering Tom Gate from the noise of St Aldate's; the stillness of the quad, the splashing of

Mercury, the rippling of the bells around the walls, through the cloisters and echoing about the Hall staircase. Oxford has never lost its magic for me. Tonight it is still as magical. The light going from the garden; blue dusk descending upon the long line of Queen's beyond. Every moment the trees grow darker; the bells are far away, ringing somewhere for evensong.'[1] Even here at All Souls, the darkness of the night shrouds the figures from history that have passed through this quad. Maybe they watch us expectantly.

Adam

Don't allow this place to smother your desires or your possibilities. It would be easy to fall into its velvet rut. It is why I wanted to escape here from Germany and my family. I want to discover myself – I have never yet found my inner being; at least not one that isn't smothered by paternal and dynastic expectations and conformities.

Rowse

I have enemies here – one's that see me as an upstart, not worthy of my place. I am determined I shall be remembered long after they are but mere footnotes of this time. So why theology at Mansfield? Was that just a reason to escape?

Adam

My frustration is that my course is short, a mere two months of relative freedom. Professor Selbie is a friend of my father's – his influence helped to get me here. Theology seemed appropriate for my values as a Christian, but I will be honest and say it was my only opportunity. I took it with relish and I am glad I did so.

Rowse

Oxford is a paradise to come back to, Adam. A friend once said to me that [2] "Oxford, like Venice, was a place to be always coming back to."[2] If you lived here all the time you would become dulled to its enchantment.

Adam

What is Mercury – the splashing of Mercury?

Rowse

A fountain at the centre of Tom Quad, Christ Church. The original reason the pond was there in the 17th century was for ready water in case of fire. It eventually became ornamental. The original Mercury statue was torn down in 1817 by Lord Derby as an undergraduate prank. A few years back a copy of Giovanni da Bologna's statue of Mercury in lead was gifted to the college as a permanent replacement.

Adam

What did you study at Christ Church?

Rowse

Can't you tell? [*he laughs to himself*] I wanted to read Literature but I was dissuaded and eventually persuaded to read History. I came as an undergraduate on a scholarship of course. I have Cornwall to thank for being here – and my Grammar School and teachers. But my intellect has always been superior, always. History is my passion. I am working on a history of the Elizabethans – an era with a great Queen and also the legacy of Shakespeare – it consumes me mostly but thankfully there are distractions.

Adam

When I first saw you across the common room at Mansfield last week, I thought you were standoffish and unapproachable. You seemed poised to rebuke or sting anyone who dare enter your personal space. Aloof, yet wanting to be engaged with. Sour of expression and yet eyes that pleaded for conversation.

Rowse

Gracious! You make me sound like one of the gargoyles.

Adam

My own destiny is unclear to me as yet. My hope is that my own
purpose will be as clear to me as you are to yours –
yours is to you, I mean. Oh, dear!

Rowse

Come on, Adam. (*he helps him to his feet*) Time for bed.

Adam

Shakespeare. I want to hear some Shakespeare
before we go, Rowse.

*Rowse looks at him and is literally enchanted by his naturalness and beauty. He
thinks for a moment as Adam watches him intently. Then in half voice he recites
a sonnet [104] to him – as he does they get up and start to exit.*

Rowse

[3] 'To me, fair friend, you never can be old,
For as you were when first your eye I eyed,
Such seems your beauty still. Three winters cold
Have from the forests shook three summers' pride,
Three beauteous springs to yellow autumn turned
In process of the seasons have I seen,
Three April perfumes in three hot Junes burned,
Since first I saw you fresh, which yet are green.
Ah, yet doth beauty, like a dial-hand,
Steal from his figure, and no pace perceived;
So your sweet hue, which methinks still doth stand,
Hath motion, and mine eye may be deceived:
For fear of which, hear this, thou age unbred:
Ere you were born was beauty's summer dead.'

They disappear up the stairs that lead to Rowse's rooms. Jackers appears with his lamp held high and watches them go. He then turns and exits.

Lights fade to blackout

Scene 3:

Sunday morning We *hear the sound of a clock nearby chiming the hour of eleven am – St Mary's Church bells peal similarly in the distance. They are all outside of the perimeter of All Souls College, Oxford.*

The lights come up on Rowse's All Souls rooms. Weak wintry light cascades through the many paned window U/S/C that looks out over the quad. We can just see the tips of other buildings in the distance.

The room is cosy and cluttered – a typical academic's study. There is a comfy chair and small sofa, all surrounded by piles of books either on ceiling height bookcases or perching precariously on side tables. A practical desk by the window is similarly cluttered. A side table has a small primus stove and kettle and other tea making paraphernalia upon it. There is a fine fireplace with overhead mantle mirror. The door S/L is the main entrance to Rowse's rooms with a coat stand at attention by its side. The door S/R leads to the bedroom and bathroom.

Once established we hear the sound of someone rushing up stone steps. The outer door bursts open and Rowse enters somewhat breathless. He is holding a bottle of milk and copies of the Sundayy Telegraph and The Sunday Times. He throws the papers onto the sofa, and crosses to the tea making table.

Rowse

Adam?

He strikes a match and lights the primus stove, shakes the kettle to check there is water in it, then places it upon the burner. It wobbles, but he steadies it with a laugh.

Rowse

Adam? Can you hear me?

He crosses to the coat stand and takes off his gown and hangs it up.

Hang the bat!

Underneath he is wearing a three piece tweed suit with shirt and tie – all fully buttoned up. His Oxford brogues gleam. He then switches on the wireless and choral music gently tickles the edges of the room.

Adam! Do you want Indian or China?

Rowse starts to add loose tea to a silver pot. He then inspects the cups and saucers and rubs them with a cloth. He opens the milk and pours some into a china milk jug.

As he does this, he fails to notice Adam emerge from the bedroom and stand by the fireplace, cigarette in hand. He leans against the mantle and watches Rowse as he exhales smoke. He is naked.

Rowse suddenly turns to ask again

Rowse

Adam, Indian or Ch…

We see his reaction flash across his face in response to Adam's naked beauty. Rowse quickly turns his back and asks again. Adam is entirely unselfconscious.

Or China?

Adam

English tea? I prefer strong coffee, if you have it, Rowse

Rowse

Sadly, no! I never use it. It creates turmoils with my indigestion.
Bugger that's hot!

*Rowse switches off the boiling kettle. Grabs a cloth and pours
the water into the pot.*

Adam

Brandy will do.

*He laughs at Rowse's expression of horror at his request for
alcohol at such an early hour.*

You English are so fucking formal. A little brandy to start the
day is no sin, Rowse.

Rowse

Indeed! I do have some actually, just for guests of course as…

Adam

It disagrees with your digestion?
My wish is that I will not have a similar effect…

*Rowse finds the brandy bottle and then a glass and pours a small medicinal
amount into the glass and hands it to Adam. He continues as if oblivious to his
nakedness.*

Rowse

I am Cornish, actually. Cornish. Not English as you say. There is a
difference, Adam.

He pours weak tea into his china cup as Adam inspects the dribble of brandy in his glass with disdain.

Adam

Are all Cornishmen as generous of spirit as you?

Rowse

Are all German's so impossibly impertinent, Adam?

Adam

Only my fellow Prussians.

Rowse

There you see, Adam! Prussian. You consider yourself to be a Prussian rather than a homogenized German. As I am a Cornishman and not an English one.

Rowse picks up the brandy bottle and fills Adam's glass with a smile.

Adam

But still so very British! And your heritage?

Rowse

I don't have one to speak of. My parents were, well, ordinary – I am technically a peasant I suppose. Derived of Cornish fishermen and clay miners. Not so glamorous is it, Adam? I think I may even be a bastard – illegitimate!

Adam

To have arrived here then, is a great achievement. History perhaps will be the better for it. Your legitimacy bothers you?

Rowse

Only in as much as I suspect my mother was fornicating with a farmer behind my father's back! Me being the result. We don't speak about it of course – actually we speak of very little. They are like aliens to me, and me to them if the truth be known. [*to change the subject*] Becoming a Fellow here was a surprise to me – my research will, as I mentioned last night, focus on the Elizabethans…for now at least.

Adam

What a waste. They are but dust – those Elizabethans. It is the here and now that should consume you – we are living in the moments that will make the history for the future.
The future of the world teeters.

Rowse

Adam, can I ask you a serious question?

Adam

Why, of course.

Rowse

Why are you naked?

Adam

Clothes are so cumbersome and I try and manage without them whenever possible. Does it bother you?

Rowse

It makes me feel uneasy – as much as I admire your Prussian physique and your liquid violet eyes. Sorry that was impertinent.

Adam crosses to the widow and stretches as he looks out. The wintry sun gives him the appearance of a Greek god.

Adam

My mother loves my eyes – I inherited them from her. That is why. I love to feel the sun caressing my skin. The light here is warm and reassuring. You are cosseted within this place. The real world barely touches you, does it?

Rowse

Oxford is only interested in my brain – it cares nothing for my body, physique or emotions. (*he looks longingly at the rear view of Adam*) Anyway, please come away from the window, Adam. If any of the older Fellows glimpse you through the window, the shock may kill them. Not to mention my reputation.

Adam

That funny little porter man in a bowler hat is looking up at the window.

Rowse

Oh, fuck! That's Jackers. Did he see you? Never mind, sit in the armchair. (*he looks around and then tosses The Sunday Times at Adam*) Here sit and read this and don't say anything. Good job it's a broadsheet…

Adam grabs the newspaper, sits in the armchair and opens it. It manages to just cover his modesty. There is a knock at the door.

Jackers (off)

Are you there, Sir?

Rowse

Yes, Jackers. Won't be a moment. (*to Adam*) Quiet.

Rowse opens the door and Jackers enters. He is holding a bundle of letters. Jackers surveys the scene. He does not bat an eyelid on seeing a naked Adam sitting reading The Times.

Jackers

Is everything all right, sir? I missed you this morning when you collected your newspapers, and you also forgot to pick up your mail yesterday. I thought I would bring it over for you.

Rowse

That's very decent of you, Jackers. Thank you kindly. You remember Herr Trott – he stayed as my guest last night.

Rowse clutches at his stomach – suddenly in considerable pain. It hits him quite hard and he cries out, much to his embarrassment.

Adam looks on slightly alarmed and goes to fold the newspaper and get up – but Jackers stops him!

Jackers

No, sir! Don't get up. (*to Rowse)* The old trouble again, sir? That reminds me, I have this for you as well. (*he pulls a blue bottle of Milk of Magnesium from his pocket and gives it him*). This will do the trick.

Rowse

Thank you, Jackers. What would I do without you. I will be fine now.

Jackers

Very well, sir. Will Herr Trott be staying for lunch?

Adam shakes his head by way of response to Rowse.

Rowse

No. No, thank you Jackers.

Jackers

Good morning to you, gentlemen.

Jackers leaves and closes the door. Rowse stumbles to the sofa and takes off the lid of the bottle and swigs the white liquid. His pain seem to subside after a moment.

Adam

Old trouble?

Rowse

The doctor thinks it could be ulcers – I am convinced it could be something worse.

Adam

The blue bottle?

Rowse

Milk of Magnesium. It is a potion concocted of thick chalky fluid, with added magnesium along with lashings of peppermint to dull the awful taste. It helps and does deaden the fire of pain somewhat.

Adam

It smells and looks disgusting.

Rowse

It is not a cure – it just temporarily distracts attention for the real problem. Like your Mr. Hitler and his National Socialists.

Adam

Prison did not destroy Hitler – just made him stronger amongst his supporters, Rowse. That is my worry for the future. Don't confuse Hitler with your brand of liberal socialism.

Rowse takes another swig of the Milk of Magnesium and regains his composure as the pain diminishes.

Rowse

I have decided to stand for parliament, you know? For the Labour Party – I can represent my Cornwall seat. The association have approved my application. It's just a matter of when, really. 1931 is the next Parliamentary General Election

Adam

To achieve what?

Rowse

I was lucky, I have been given a chance and opportunities to make something of my life. Everyone should have those opportunities, if they are capable.

Adam

What if they are not – capable?

Rowse

There should also be a better distribution of the country's resources – free health and pensions for the elderly. The aristocracy have had it too good for too long. It's just not fair.

Adam

There is no such thing as fairness, Rowse. Money is the god of capitalism. Power controls fascism and communism, they stroll hand in hand with fear and oppression. It's just that nobody knows it yet. But they will.

Rowse stands and moves to the fireplace, he winces in pain and still holds his stomach. Adam suddenly gets up and crosses to him.

Rowse

I think I am going to die, Adam.

Adam takes hold of Rowse's tie and pulls it free of his waistcoat. He begins to untie it slowly and seductively. Rowse is transfixed and unnerved at Adam's naked closeness.

Adam

You can't die, Rowse.
How can you die when you have never lived?

He pulls his tie free and tosses it across the room.
Adam is so close Rowse can feel his breath.

Can you smell me Rowse? Can you smell that odour of desire and longing? Do you want to feel my skin? Feel the life rushing through my veins. The passion I have in my soul? How close that line must now be between restraint and submission. Think of the joy you could experience if you would just cross that line. The relief, the joy to let all that passion out of your trussed up life. You are a tight as the tweed suit you are encased in. The only thing stiff, that British upper lip! Discard it Rowse, discard it.

Rowse suddenly finds himself and pushes away from Adam. He rushes into the bedroom and returns holding Adam's trousers with braces still attached. He hands them to him

Rowse

I've never been intimate – properly – in a sexual way. Please encumber yourself of these trousers. Auden made a pass at me once, it perplexed me terribly. He still can't look me in the eye. Nor me him, with ease.

Adam

I can look you in the eye, Rowse.

Adam crosses to him and in a flash kisses him on the lips. He then puts his trousers on and lifts the braces over his shoulders.

Live, Rowse. Start to live!

Adam exits to the bedroom. Rowse turns up the radio - Al Bowlly appear as he sings Close Your Eyes

Close Your Eyes

Rowse smiles to himself and picks up his discarded tie.
Without thinking he puts it back on but leaves the top button of his
shirt undone and the tie lose at the neck.

Adam *(off)*

Rowse? Can you come here a minute.

Rowse looks at himself in the mirror and smiles wickedly at himself. He then
exits to the bedroom slightly apprehensively.

Lights fade on room and up on:

Al Bowlly as he continues to sing Close Your Eyes

Close Your Eyes

The lights slowly fade to blackout.

Music (instrumental) continues for scene and time change.

Scene 4:

A few weeks later. The lights come up on Rowse's rooms at All Souls. It is
empty. The side table lamps are on and there is a glow from a small fire burning
in the grate.

The bells of Saint Mary's Church begin to ring the hour of 6pm.

Rowse enters clutching some letters. He takes his coat and gown off and hangs
them up on the stand. He suddenly stops and looks around the room as if
searching for something. He throws the letters on the desk, then crosses to the fire
and warms his hands. Going back to the desk, he sits and looks at one of the
letters and stares at it – it remains unopened but he knows it is from Adam.
Rowse writes an entry in his diary: (he can relay this as his thoughts to the
audience)

Rowse

My mind is so distracted, Adam. Thanks to you I should say. Everywhere I go and everything I do brings me back to you and those violet eyes! I feel like I am being pulled into a vortex of your making and it is eating me up. I have tried walking for miles to make my mind think of anything but you and your terrible but beautiful influence on me. I never realized I possessed what people called emotions until you wrenched them out of my insides. Now there is nothing but this hollow void you left behind. Everywhere I look [*he looks around the room*] seems bereft of your presence – your vitality. How is Germany, Adam? How is life for you? Do you even realize I am not in your daily life anymore? No doubt you are probably fucking someone else. I shouldn't care very much, should I? Trouble is, I do. I really do, Adam. I do care and I hate you for it as much as I love you for it. No turning back now, Adam. The flame has been lit and it can never be extinguished. A student asked me today to explain some obvious trifle concerning Queen Elisabeth the first. As I looked into his expectant, youthful face all I could think about was you. The old Queen and all I know of her deserted me and I began to feel like a fool. For a moment I was horrified to think his lips might be yours and I would kiss them. Can you imagine? Can you?

There is a knock at the door that breaks Rowse's reverie and brings his attention back to reality.

Rowse

Yes?

His friend Vickers enters in a great bluster – he is like an enthusiastic puppy and full of sincerity and charm.
He immediately senses that Rowse is out of sorts somewhat.

Vickers

Hello, old man. Where have you been the last few days? I missed our chats and disemboweling the Elizabethan psychology! I asked at the Bodleian if they had seen you and they said no. I can't believe it – are you ill old man?

Rowse

For heaven's sake Vickers stop prattling on. And I am not old for God's sake! Sorry, unintended blasphemy. My apologies.

Vickers

Apology accepted..

Rowse

You will have us old before our time, Vickers. I am only 27 and you are only 28 if I remember rightly?

Vickers

Oh, yes! I do believe I am, although I feel much older sometimes almost prehistoric first thing in the morning.

Rowse

(*laughing*) Yes, mornings never are your strong point. Bit of a disadvantage for a Vicar in waiting.

Vickers

God will give me the strength I need on the mornings I need it, Rowse. You'll see. Besides I am happy being Curate in the chapel here ad infinitum or whatever…

Rowse

He won't like you yawning in the pulpit – it will dilute your sermons a tad dear boy.

Vickers

I say, "dear boy", don't think anyone has called me that since my mother. I think I prefer old man after all.

Rowse

Indeed! Sorry but I have been busy with one thing and another and I am afraid my research has gone to pot these last weeks. Terrible, I know, but there you have it.

Vickers

You're not ill or anything – I know you have stomach problems occasionally, but there is nothing else?

Rowse

No, nothing physical anyway.

Vickers

Oh, dear.

Rowse

What is that supposed to mean?

Vickers

Forgive me for prying but this hasn't got anything to do with that Adam Trott chap has it. He turned heads everywhere, and all I can see is that he left devastation in his wake! He's gone back to Germany I understand so at least the ripples in the pond will eventually run themselves out..

Rowse

How very astute of you. Why would you think my mood had anything to do with Adam?

Vickers

You see? First name terms – you said Adam! I knew it was something to do with him. After all you did spend quite a bit of time together didn't you? I am not blind you know, Rowse. Some of the older Fellows didn't approve of you fraternizing with him – him being German and all. They still bubble and boil with rage over the war you know.

Rowse

We have to move on. Not all Germans are bad and the war ended a dozen years ago come November. If more Germans thought as Adam did then the world would be a better place eventually. They are not all like this new fellow, Mr. Hitler!

Vickers

First name terms and defending him! You have got it bad my friend. Do you want to talk about it? We Homos need to stick together at least.

Rowse

Please don't use that expression it makes me feel uncomfortable. Anyway, since when have you been a Homo as you put it?

Vickers

Mostly in my head actually, but I hope to divert it to a physical experience if anyone becomes willing.

Rowse

Well, don't look at me will you!

Vickers

Gracious, no! I couldn't even imagine such a prospect, Rowse. You are a friend. That's all you'll ever be to me.

Rowse

No sure if I am pleased, relieved or offended!

Vickers

Although, one day I will of course get married to a suitable woman who will be a perfect Vicar's wife. That's my duty and my destiny. I suppose I shall manage whatever is required of me in, er…that way…

Rowse

Bugger that! I have been called a misogynistic bastard before now. I'll stick with that. Women unnerve me and I am not keen to be around them much. I prefer to stick with intellectuals. Much safer and less stressful for one's constitution.

Vickers

You have it bad, don't you? This German chap has got to you, hasn't he? He stayed here a few nights in your rooms, did you…

Rowse

Vickers! That's none of your business. Anyway, how do you know he stayed overnight with me? Have you been spying on me?

Vickers

Of course not. It's common knowledge among the porters and other Fellows. You are the gossip of the moment – or at least you were whilst he was still here.

Rowse

They should have better things to do than spend their time discussing me and my friends.

Vickers

You didn't answer my question. How bad is it?

Rowse

Awful. I miss him terribly and I can't focus or concentrate on anything. I have tried everything. I have walked, even sort of run in a trotting kind of fashion, but all to no avail. I cannot read, write or even sleep without visions of him invading my mind and dominating it. What am I to do, Vickers?

Vickers

I cannot believe I am about to say this, Rowse. Sounds like you are in love. Really in love with him. That is taking things too, too far dear boy.

Rowse

What do you mean?

Vickers

Well, its okay being a Homo among friends but its nothing more than a bit of a kiss and cuddle. But you don't do love, that is very dangerous and to be avoided at all costs. After all, we have to get married eventually and it just complicates things for later life.

Rowse

Sometimes Vickers, you say the most absurdly truthful nonsense. It takes my breath away. I shall never marry, of course. My mind is made up on that score. I will not build a false façade of respectability. Anyway, why should two men who love each other not be able to live happily together. Maybe that needs to change along with outdated and draconian laws that make our sexuality illegal.

Vickers

Criminal offence in the eyes of the law. I certainly have no intention of going to prison for anyone. If you mind my advice, Rowse, as a friend, forget about Adam, forget about any thoughts of love, just get on with your life and do what you do best.

Rowse

Bugger the law!

Vickers

I think that may be what is called a contradiction in terms!

Rowse

Sometimes Vickers, you make my head hurt.

Vickers

That's nothing to what I do to my own – no wonder I get headaches.

Rowse

Anyway, the die is cast. I received this letter from Adam this morning. I have been too afraid to open it. How pathetic.

Vickers

Well there is only one way to find out what he has to say isn't there? I shall leave you to it then. But remember what I said. I will see you later at Chapel perhaps?

Rowse

Perhaps. If not I will see you at dinner tonight.

Vickers leaves. Rowse's head is full of thoughts after their discussion. He crosses to the desk and picks up Adam's unopened letter and looks at it almost as if he is afraid of it. He sits in the armchair and rips it open and begins to read it. He then starts to write in his diary again – he speaks his thoughts as he writes – addressing the audience:

Rowse

[4] 'Today there came a letter from him: it seems he has been filled with thoughts of me all these last days as I of him. A strange providence that led to that crossing of our paths: could I have known, or he, that we should make such an impression on each other? It seems incredible that it ever should have happened; it might easily have not, and life would be infinitely the poorer. At the moment it makes me happy to have my love returned in that un-dreamed of way. When he wrote, it was for the same reasons that haunts my mind: he could not hold onto what he called the 'adventure' of the soul that night, and I the 'experience'. He feared he might forget and asks for some pictures to remember me by. He says 'our souls loved each other' in that hour. It's a distressing experience,

35

which for my part I am prepared to go through with, though it can bring only unhappiness in the end. He can never hold to love for me: we can ultimately make nothing of it [– can we?] So I happily give him perfect freedom: he can rest assured of my devotion to the memory.'

The emotion and his sense of loss is too great for him to bear and he breaks down in tears.

We hear Al Bowlly singing The Very Thought of You

The lights cross fade – out on Rowse and up on Al Bowlly as he sings.

The Very Thought of You

The lights fade to blackout.

Segue to Radio Broadcast :

Scene 5

Trinity Term 1931
Rowse's Rooms – All Souls - Afternoon

A radio news broadcast on the BBC is heard.

BBC Announcer (female)

Bringing you Al Bowlly on the Light Programme.
We now go to the newsroom for some breaking news.

BBC News Announcer (male)

This is the BBC news from London. It has just been announced that Herr Hitler of Germany has confirmed he is to challenge Hindenburg for the Presidency. Many believe that Hitler's National Socialist party's electoral success has spurred him to make this move. He increased the seats held by the Nazis in the German Parliament from 14 to 107 in last year's election. Will 1931 see a new German President? We will bring you an update on the 6 o'clock news.

Segue to the Savoy Orpheans Orchestra who continue to play the orchestral version of The Very Thought of You.

The lights come up on Rowse's Rooms – Radio continues but fades under

After a moment Jackers enters followed by Lady Price and her daughter Veronica. Lady Price is a charming but determined woman and typical of her class. She is forthright and obviously embarrasses her daughter. Their individual characters are immediately revealed to us by the way they react to Rowse's somewhat eclectic, untidy study. Lady Price looks around slightly alarmed that dust is in evidence and the untidiness of his books, whereas Veronica is enthralled by the atmosphere of academia and education.

Jackers

I do apologise your Ladyship but Mr. Rowse has not yet returned from Christ Church. He is expected presently.

Lady Price

I suppose this will do. (*she runs a finger disdainfully across a pile of dusty books*) Better than waiting in that awful, draughty porter's lodge.

Veronica

Mother! Please don't make such a fuss.

Jackers

Can I get your ladyship some tea, perhaps?

Lady Price

No. However, you could turn that awful noise off. Fancy wasting electricity letting a wireless play away to itself. The Light Programme as well!

Jackers crosses and switches the radio off. Veronica is enthralled by all the books. She immediately feels at home in this room.

Veronica

I would like some tea if that's possible, Mr. Jackers.

Lady Price

Oh, Veronica you are impossible. You would deliberately say yes if I said no – and vice versa just to spite me.

Veronica

I'm sorry, but I am quite thirsty and it will pass the time until Mr. Rowse gets here.

Jackers

China or Indian ?

Veronica

I prefer an ordinary afternoon blend if you have it. Is that possible?

Lady Price

I despair sometimes at your lack of taste, Veronica. I may as well join you if you are having some.

Jackers

Very well madam – your Ladyship. Please excuse me.

Jackers exits

Lady Price

Well I think it is very rude that Mr. Rowse has failed to meet us at the arranged time. Worse we are treated like some kind of grocer being made to wait in a porter's lodge. Disgraceful. Wait until your father hears about this. He will have second thoughts about you coming to a place like this once he does.

Veronica

For goodness sake, mother. Don't you find the atmosphere here thrilling? Can't you feel the history and the possibilities?

Lady Price

The what? I do know the dust in this room is terrible. I am surprised it isn't making me cough. You know how much I loathe dust!

Veronica

Please sit down. The dust won't hurt you – think about your blood pressure.

Lady Price dusts a seat of the sofa with her handkerchief. She sits gingerly on the edge with as much decorum as she can muster. Veronica has pulled a book from the shelf and is reading it.

Lady Price

It simply baffles me why you would want to subject yourself to this. What did education ever bring a young woman of your station. It is a suitable marriage you should be looking for...

Veronica

Please don't start that again. How many times must I tell you I am not interested in marriage.

Lady Price

Well you should be, darling. You should be. You don't want to end up an old maid, do you?

Veronica

I am 21! For goodness sake stop being so hysterical...

Lady Price is about to retort indignantly when Jackers enters with a tray of tea. He crosses to the desk and puts the tray down. He then begins to set out cups and saucers to serve them.

Lady Price

We will discuss this later – in private.

Jackers

Milk or lemon, your ladyship?

Lady Price

At this hour, lemon. (*as an afterthought*) Please.

Veronica

Milk for me *please*, Mr. Jackers.

Lady Price

Will the illusive Mr. Rowse appreciate you touching his books, Veronica. Its quite impolite when you haven't even asked.

Veronica

I am sure he won't mind, after all if he is going to be my History tutor I need to understand his taste. Fascinating it is too!

Jackers hands Lady Price her tea. He then hands Veronica hers.

Jackers

Would you like sugar?

Lady Price raises her hand to decline as if she cannot find words to describe what she thinks of him for asking. Veronica sighs with impatience at her mother then smiles at Jackers.

Veronica

No, thank you. We are fine now Mr. Jackers.

Jackers

If you need me I shall be in the porter's lodge. As soon as Mr. Rowse returns I will let him know you are waiting. Good day.

Jackers exits and closes the door behind himself.

Lady Price

I still can't believe your father agreed to you coming up to Oxford. However, Lady Margaret Hall is a nice college and you will have rooms there so I know you are safe at least.

Veronica

Never mind. One day I will think about getting married. There is much more to life first, so much to discover…

Lady Price

When I was a girl we did not have any other choice. It was a good marriage or nothing. Otherwise poverty and destitution beckoned!

Veronica

What rot! Your idea of poverty is not having enough dresses or furs or diamonds. Think of all those who lost everything in the Wall Street Crash – many through no fault of their own. That's real poverty.

Lady Price

All the things you mention seem wholly more appealing than being stuck in Oxford amongst all these stuffy old men – yes, Veronica, old men. Where in that environment is there any life? I am sorry, darling girl, but it all seems an utter waste of time to me. One has to think of one's future.

Veronica

Oh, please, Mother don't start using that affected manner of speaking. One this and one that! The future for us all is starting to feel rather precarious indeed. Do you ever listen to the news? The world is one the edge and I am determined to be part of its salvation.

I am glad the world doesn't have to rely on you saving it.

Lady Price

That is twice today you have been impertinent. Impertinence is very unattractive in a young woman. Very. I shall speak to your father of course. Not that it will do any good.

Veronica has become engrossed in reading one of Rowse's books.

Are you even listening to me, Veronica?

The All Souls clock chimes the hour of 3 O'clock. The sound resonates gently into the atmosphere of the room and renders Lady Price silent for a moment at least. Veronica continues reading.

What are you reading?

Veronica

It's called Mein Kampf.

Lady Price

My what? Does it mean anything in English?

Veronica

It translates as 'My Struggle'.

Lady Price

By whom? Who would write such a dreary sounding book.

Veronica

Adolf Hitler…

Lady Price

I have heard that name before – on the news I think.

Veronica

Bravo, mother - you are not completely isolated from the world then. Adolf Hitler is a German politician, the one ruffling all the feathers at the moment. From what I have read his book is somewhat radical.

She puts the book down and picks another off the shelf and looks at it intently. There is a noise outside that grabs their attention. We hear Rowse's voice and then hurried footsteps approach

Rowse (off)

Thank you Jackers, I am on my way…

Rowse bursts into his rooms slightly breathless. He beams a smile at Lady Price and completely disarms her.

Rowse

Lady Price, I am delighted to meet you at last. (*he kisses her hand*) Please accept my apologies there was a matter of life and death at Christ Church. One of my old tutors was sadly taken ill and I had to cover his lecture at short notice – the reason I am late.

Lady Price

Of course I understand, Mr. Rowse. (*she giggles girlishly*) I am sorry but you are much younger than I imagined you would be. Veronica why didn't you tell me…

Rowse smiles then looks at Veronica and the book she is holding.

Rowse

I see you have an interest in German history. 'Forty Years After. The Story of the Franco-German War' by HC Bailey, published in 1914. He was an Oxford man you know. Writes crime fiction now – third-rate sadly.

Lady Price

Doesn't he also write for the Daily Telegraph? I suppose you think my novels are also third-rate, Mr. Rowse?

Rowse and Veronica stop talking and look at her in surprise

Rowse

Yes he does, Lady Price, write for the Telegraph. I haven't read any of your novels…

Veronica steers Rowse back into her conversation. Lady Price takes her compact out and tidies her hair and checks her lipstick.

Veronica

Father didn't approve of mother writing novels – he said to me if you are going to write, write about history. That sealed my fate and aroused my passion. It's why I am here.

Lady Price

My novels were a hobby really – nothing serious and probably as you say, third-rate. But at least I have no pretensions about them or myself…

Rowse is about to respond when Veronica cuts in quickly to distract him from her mother's sarcasm

Veronica

Anyway, Mr.Rowse, you could argue that the unification of Germany at the end of the war in 1871 led to the Great War, and also to the current unrest in Germany.

Rowse

Well it did give the world the Kaiser – so there was certainly reason to believe that too much power was generated by Bismarck's unification. The Prussian dominance has struggled to find a voice under the status quo for certain.

Veronica

The twenty sixth of February 1871 changed the course of history. Versailles, and treaties signed there, have been a thorn in Germany's side more than once.

Rowse

And continue to be so.

Veronica

Hitler's success seems to be riding the crest of the same populist wave then. In Mein Kampf he says that he believes "Anything miserable, weak or cowardly must be eradicated, having no compassion or pity [with anything] that does not conform to his ideals." Does he mean that in a literal way?

Rowse

Let's hope not.

She picks up Mein Kampf and looks at it thoughtfully

Veronica

How can Herr Hitler be so awful, and if he is why are so
Many people voting for him. Who is Adam?

Rowse

I beg your pardon?

Veronica

I noticed the dedication in the front of the book.
'To Rowse from Adam.'

There is an awkward silence.

Lady Price

Veronica! What have I told you about impertinence?

Rowse

No, please, I am not offended. Adam is a friend, a German friend,
and he sent me that copy so I could see why he considered Hitler
such a threat to his country.

Veronica

For someone so reviled, Hitler seems to be making
extraordinary gains in German politics. We have family in
Germany you know.

Rowse

No, I didn't know.
Your interest is for European history then?

Veronica

Goodness no! Give me the seventeenth century any day! The Stuarts, a chopping block, a civil war and the Restoration! That's my passion. I hope to research that era during my studies at Lady Margaret Hall.

Rowse

How very refreshing, I can see why we get along so splendidly and I will look forward to seeing you again in Michaelmas Term. I may however be a couple of weeks late back due to the General Election in October.

Lady Price

Why?

Rowse

I am standing as a Parliamentary Candidate in the election for my Cornwall constituency of Falmouth

Lady Price

For the Conservatives?

Rowse

No, as a Labour candidate.

Lady Price

Oh, I see…

Veronica

Thank you for agreeing to be my History Tutor. I will look forward to seeing you later in the year. I hope if you win that election I shall still get to see you?

Rowse

We shall cross that bridge if we come to it.

Lady Price.

Would you care to join us for dinner at the Randolph tonight, Mr. Rowse. My husband would, I know, be delighted to see you. And as you and Veronica obviously hit it off so well, she would enjoy your company no doubt.

Veronica

Mother, I am sure Mr. Rowse is busy…

Rowse is taken off guard but after a moment he smiles.

Rowse

I would be delighted.

Lady Price

That's settled then. Dinner is at eight.
Nothing too formal. Black tie, of course.

Rowse

Of course. I shall look forward to it. Perhaps we can continue our discussion at dinner, Veronica?

Veronica

Thank you.

Lady Price

Come along now, Veronica. I need to rest a while as it
has been an exhausting day. Good day, Mr.Rowse.

*Lady Price glides out with a smile. Veronica holds back a little and then speaks
to Rowse once she is out of earshot.*

Veronica

I am sorry, Mr. Rowse, but my mother seems set on matchmaking.
She assumed you were old, now she sees you as marriage material –
even though you are a socialist and member of the Labour Party!

Rowse

How can you tell?

Veronica

She invited you for dinner!

*Veronica exits quickly. Rowse chuckles to himself having thoroughly enjoyed the
encounter in an odd way. He picks up the book that Adam gave him and looks
at the inscription.*

*After a few moments there is a knock at the door. Rowse sighs in expectation of a
reprise of Lady Price and Veronica*

Rowse

Enter.

His friend Vickers comes in and is obviously desperate to impart some news

Vickers

Hello, old man. Am I disturbing you?

Rowse

No. No, not at all Vickers. What can I do for you?
Do you want to sit down, you look flushed...

Vickers

Do I? I must have been running - so great was my
haste to get here and tell you

Rowse

Well?

Vickers

I have been over at Balliol College to give a talk and I bumped into a
friend and he told me something that will interest you greatly.
Apparently they have restored the German Rhodes Scholarship for
the first time since the Great War. Guess who they have awarded it
to, to study PPE? It's a great honour. Adam!

Rowse

Well, that is marvelous news. I can't understand though why he never
told me of his application.

Vickers

Come on, Rowse. He always said he would come
back and study properly at Oxford. Perhaps he didn't want to
tell you in case he didn't get it.

Rowse

Perhaps.

Vickers

I thought you would be thrilled...

Rowse

Yes, of course I am. I am delighted for Adam. It's just I can't imagine having him around again – and the implications of it I suppose.

Vickers

You need to forget about any thoughts of love, Rowse. That will lead to problems.

Rowse

Forget? There are only two people in this world I love, Vickers. One of them is my mother, the other is Adam von Trott.

We hear the Savoy Orpheans playing an instrumental version of The Very Thought of You!

Scene 6

The lights cross fade – out on Rowse and Vickers and up on Adam in Germany. He sits at his desk writing a letter to Rowse. He wears only a pair of white silk pajama bottoms and monogrammed slippers. He speaks his thoughts aloud to the audience:

Adam

My dear Rowse. I am beyond excited to tell you that I have been accepted at Balliol to study Politics, Philosophy and Economics! That they also awarded me the scholarship is also a great honour and will make the finances a little easier. How wonderful to think I shall be able to spend two whole years in Oxford! That I will be able to study amongst my friends and you in the city that has enchanted me. My third year I have decided to spend in the United States as I want to really understand how the world works and what I can contribute to its future. Enough of me, Rowse. How are preparations going for the election in October? Imagine if you won and became a member of parliament? The doors that would open for us. The information we could be privy to, information that would help us change the world.

No doubt you have heard about Hitler's attempt to steal the Presidency from Hindenburg? He did not succeed this time, but he will I have no doubt. My fear, Rowse, is that Hitler and his Nazis are becoming unstoppable.

A young woman enters and drapes her arm around Adam.
She is wearing only a white silk underslip

Adam (cont)

I must go now, Rowse. Please write with your news and the election campaign. I cannot wait to see you in Oxford for Michaelmas Term. My love to you always.

He quickly folds the letter and puts in an envelope and seals it.

The music swells and Adam takes the young woman in his arms and kisses her passionately. They then begin to dance seductively as the music crescendos. As they do a Nazi flag unfurls behind them. The sound of Hitler ranting at a public Nazi rally drowns out the music creating discord.

Interval

Other People's Fu**ing!

Act Two

Scene 1
October 1931
Election Count – Cornwall

*The lights come up on Rowse standing by a blackboard that has the final votes for
each candidate chalked onto the board.*

Conservative: 16,388
Liberal: 14,006
Labour: 10,098

*He looks somewhat forlorn and still has his red Labour rosette pinned
to the lapel of his tweed suit. Rowse loosens his tie and then pulls off his rosette
and stuffs it inside his jacket pocket. His friend Vickers enters.*

Vickers

Never mind, Rowse, you didn't win but you gave them a bloody
nose. Better luck next time. The consolation, if the rumours are true,
is that Ramsay Macdonald will be PM in a coalition.

Rowse

Never mind? I came third, Vickers! I have never been third-rate or a
loser in my life until now, and I hate it. Its humiliating.

Vickers

You are not any of those things – you were up against an almost impossible task. You need to take the positives from this. I also suggest you grow a thicker skin if you are to be involved in politics. It's a dirty business.

Rowse

Have they all gone?

Vickers

Yes – just. The Association Chairman said he will call you when the dust has settled.

Rowse

Indeed he will. No doubt a post-mortem will be in order. Vickers, take that rosette off now. You have done your bit – and I do appreciate your help these last two days.

Vickers

My pleasure, old man. I have found it quite thrilling, never having been to a General Election count before. Its all very formal, and seeing the men in suits hovering in the shadows is quite mysterious.

Rowse

They are the vultures from the Establishment, ready to whisk you away if you get elected.

Vickers

Will we be driving back to Oxford this evening?

Rowse

Yes. Quicker we put this behind us and get back to reality the better.
You go and get some sleep and I will see you later.

*We hear the BBC News radio announcer confirming that
the Conservatives have won the election.*

BBC News Announcer

Labour's Ramsay Macdonald wishes to form a National Government
– a coalition between the Conservatives and the Labour Party -
and is attending the Palace to speak to the King. It is expected that
His Majesty will instruct Macdonald to form a government. In spite
of the landslide vote for the Conservatives, the new coalition
government will be headed by Prime Minister Ramsay Macdonald.
More details on the main news at 6pm this evening.

*The newscaster fades out and we hear an instrumental version
of Al Bowlly's Blue Moon for the scene and time change.*

Scene 2
Bodleian Quad – November Evening - 1931

*As the lights come up, it is a late, misty evening a few days later in the quad of
the Bodleian Library. The statue of William Herbert stares imperiously down.
We hear a clock chime the hour of seven o'clock. After a moment we see Adam
appear – he has been standing behind the plinth of the statue but comes into view.
He is waiting.*

Once established the music fades out

*A couple of tutors and students scurry past, gowns flapping in their wake. Two
young women come out of one of the library doors – Veronica and her friend
Diana. They pass the statue and then Veronica recognizes Adam.*

Veronica

Hello, Adam? What are you waiting around for?
You're not lost are you?

Adam

No, I am not. Just waiting for a friend.

Diana

Hello.

*Adam smiles at Diana warmly. She reciprocates but
without much confidence.*

Veronica

Sorry! How rude of me. Adam this is my friend, Diana.
She is also at Lady Margaret Hall. Diana this is Adam von Trott, a
friend of Rowse my tutor.

Diana

Pleased to meet you, Herr Trott. I share your German heritage –
through my grandmother's family. Berlin.

Adam

What are you studying?

Diana

Politics, philosophy and economics.

Veronica

Another one with political and socialist ideals, Adam. (*to Diana*)
Adam's here on a Rhodes Scholarship at Balliol, also reading PPE!
You will get along famously I'm sure.

Diana

Have you settled in well, Adam?

Adam

Yes, thank you. I am not a stranger to Oxford – I have been here
before a couple of years ago. It feels familiar, like home. (*almost to
himself*) You can hear the heart beat of the past - and history in this
place.

Veronica

Indeed. Sorry, Adam but enough of this chit-chat. We are due back at
Halls for a fresher's dinner at eight. We'll have to skip to make it in
time, Diana.

Adam.

Of course, don't let me keep you. I take a stroll to Angel Meadow
most mornings – I may see you there, if you would like?

Diana

I never heard of it –

Adam

On the other side of Magdalen Bridge – just past the Half Moon
public house and turn left and walk through the trees – the meadow
lies beyond.

Veronica

Diana, come along now. Thank you, Adam, see you soon.

They exit but not before Diana has glanced back at Adam. She then skips off to catch up with Veronica.

Adam

Goodbye.

After they have gone Adam shivers and pulls his coat tighter around him to keep the cold out. He lights a cigarette and then looks at his watch to check the time. He seems resigned to leave but just as he has the thought his friend appears.

Adam

Rowse? I have been waiting for you.
I always seem to be waiting.

Rowse

Hello, Adam. Why? Is there an emergency?

Adam

Only in that I worried why my dearest friend was
perhaps avoiding me?

Rowse

Don't be absurd. Why would I avoid you?
Have you settled in at Balliol?

Adam

Yes, thank you. My rooms are nice but I had forgotten how terribly cold and damp it can be at this time of the year! The small fire grate does little to alleviate the problem.

Rowse

Once you have been here a few weeks you will acclimatize to the damp and cold. Everyone feels it at first – especially this time of year. Keep yourself wrapped up.

Adam

I prefer not to be, Rowse, as you well know…

Rowse

Stop trying to beguile me. Attempting to conjure up images of your nakedness is a bit low – even for you.

Adam

I cannot believe that, Rowse.

A couple hurry past. They hug and kiss as they go.

Rowse

See what I mean, Adam. We are trying to change the world and make it a better place for the likes of them. I fear we waste our time. They are third-rate people and not worth speaking to – never mind saving.

Adam

Why are you so angry? The kindness has gone from your voice. That makes me sad. Is it because you lost the election?

Rowse

You ask too many questions – one's that at the moment I am too tired to think about answering. I have missed you terribly you know. Of course you do.

Adam

I have missed being close to you.
Our souls need each other to survive.

Rowse

You do talk utter rot at times, Adam. We come into this world alone and we will depart it equally alone.

Adam

No. You are wrong. There is no going back now for us.
Our fates will be forever entwined. You just have to trust life.
Trust me.

Rowse

Well at this moment I am cold, tired and rather bad tempered as a result. If you want to walk with me on your way back to Balliol, you are welcome. As for trusting you? You are as yet unaware, as I am, that your Prussian ego will always be the dominant force in your life.

Adam

My ego would rather come with you to All Souls.

Do you have the same rooms there?

Rowse

If you must, then come along. But I promise nothing but
my intellect – superior as it is.

Adam

Our time apart has done nothing to help your frigidness, Rowse.
Your letters were so witty and chatty – they belied the oppressions
you happily subject yourself to.

Rowse

My letters, I fear, played a charade and told you only what you
wanted to hear. I am sure had you retained your common sense you
would have interpreted them differently.

Rowse starts to exit – Adam follows him.

*We hear Blue Moon. Towards the end of the introduction section the lights fade
out and then up on Al Bowlly who sings the song.*

Blue Moon

*The lights come up on Rowse's rooms and we see them enter. Rowse hangs up his
gown and then switches on the side table lamps. Adam throws off his coat and
jacket and loosens his shirt. He crosses to the fireplace and then removes Rowse's
jacket, waistcoat and tie. Rowse makes a pretence of objection. Adam then grabs
him and they begin to dance to the song.*

Blue Moon

*Al Bowlly fades away. The instrumental version continues as Rowse and Adam
dance together in their solitude. Rowse clutches his stomach in pain. Adam helps*

him to the sofa and hands him a bottle of Milk of Magnesium. Rowse drinks it as the lights slowly fade to blackout, the sound of Hitler addressing a rally swamps the music. Chants of "Zieg Heil" are repeated and become louder.

Lights fade out on Al Bowlly

Scene 3
All Souls – Rowse's Rooms - Hilary Term – 1933

Veronica and Diana are waiting in Rowse's rooms at All Souls. It is afternoon. Diana is sitting in the armchair reading the Daily Telegraph, Veronica is standing by the window – Jackers is standing in the doorway, bowler hat in hand.

Veronica

Thank you Mr. Jackers. We are quite happy to wait.

Jackers

Mr. Rowse asked me to offer his apologies in any case. He also asked me to tell you that Herr Trott is with him and they will be here as soon as they can – trains willing! Can I get you anything, ladies?

Veronica

Nothing for me. Diana?

Diana

No, thank you.

Jackers

If you need me I will be in the porter's lodge.

Veronica

Splendid!

She smiles at him warmly. Jackers exits.
Veronica crosses and sits on the sofa.

Diana

There is of course much talk about a policy of appeasement with Hitler. Most people see that as preferable I think to another war.

Veronica

Most people? Some people I think would be a better analysis. I am not sure I see the point really. If Hitler is as bad as some suggest, then it is probable that attempting to appease him would be futile.

Diana

They say that Hitler will be made Chancellor of Germany eventually – it seems inevitable according to the papers.

Veronica

Oh, I do hope not.

Diana

Why? Maybe it will not be as bad as people think it will. After all, the German economy is doing well and there is, apparently, a sense of optimism in Germany that hasn't been apparent since the end of the last war.

Veronica

Maybe it is all an illusion as Adam said last week. He seems to think that Hitler will be a disaster for Germany – that he will destroy the decency and spirit of the true Germany.

Diana

The thing that bothers me, to be honest, is the reports that the Jews are being blamed for all the economic ills of Germany. It seems odd.

Veronica

You feel that because you are Jewish – or at least have a Jewish ancestry – but all those people who are not Jewish will care little. They will be glad that the spotlight is not on them. When things go wrong, people always look to blame someone...

Diana

It is absurd propaganda anyway. There are far too many Jews in high ranking positions in Germany – some of the biggest manufacturers, retailers and bankers are all Jewish. The country couldn't function if they were all banished somehow. Besides, where would they go?

Veronica

I see what you mean, but for me it is a far more complex situation than we give it credit. Hitler, I believe, is on a mission to create the equivalent of the British Empire. He certainly seems to want to control mainland Europe.

Diana

In Mein Kampf he talks about a master race – true Arian blood and all that. Is it possible to modify a nation by controlling genetics. What happens to those who are not Arian and thus less than perfect?

Veronica

Like the universe, the more I think about its infinity, the more worried and uneasy I become. Hitler has the same effect on me.

Diana

Adam is utterly convinced that Hitler will be the downfall of the world. He is frightened that Germany, and true Germans as he calls them, like himself, must do everything they can to save the honour of his country and convince other governments that not everyone supports Hitler's rise.

Veronica

As a German Baron, perhaps he is better placed than most to champion that cause. Alas, I feel that perhaps many will be deaf to his protestations until the situation worsens. The question I ask is will Adam be your downfall?

Diana

We have fun but that is all. I also know I am one of many! But it is impossible for me not to love him in spite of it all.

Veronica

It's all a mystery to me this business of love. It bypasses me, and probably very wisely. Do you have regrets about leaving after your first year?

Diana

No, honestly not. Academia was not for me. I found all the research and essays rather boring if I am frank. I wanted to get out into the world and earn some money.

Veronica

I admire your honesty. And I am pleased we have stayed friends and that you spend so much time here.

Diana

My parents don't admire me for dropping out. They think I am a fool and deserve everything I get. Its not hard staying in touch with you all really – seeing Adam is also not a great chore either. I will the week days away so I can get the train here every weekend.

Veronica

You do spend a lot of time together, so I hear…

Diana

Hear from whom?

Veronica

You, mostly. You never stop talking about him.

Diana

Oh, dear! Am I that annoying?

Veronica

It has nothing to do with me, Diana, and I love you dearly as a friend. But, just be careful. I don't want to see you hurt or anything. From where I am standing, Adam seems to be more in love with himself and his ideals than he ever will be with anyone else.

Diana

I know. I am not a complete fool, Veronica. But I am smitten.

Veronica

You are not alone – there are a few broken hearts around Oxford as a result of Adam's charms.

Diana

I know that too, but I am still smitten. Did I tell you the story of our trip to the top of Magdalen Tower the other morning at dawn?

Veronica

No, but I fear you are going to…

Diana

As my cousin is a Fellow at Magdalen, he has keys to the tower. Adam and I had talked all night, and as dawn was breaking we got the key and climbed to the top to watch the sunrise over Oxford. Oh, Veronica it was so mystical – we felt like two deities surveying their Kingdom. The mist, the sunlight bathing the honey stoned colleges accompanied by the striking of bells and clocks everywhere. It was a moment I shall never forget as long as I live. I wanted to kiss Adam to make it perfect, but he chose that moment to tell me that he could never love anyone – only Germany.

Veronica

How tiresome of him…

Diana

Not at all. He only said what I already knew – besides he has said it before to me. I know the score you see, Veronica. I still love him though, probably more so because of it. If he were gushing and declaring undying I should find it boring and insincere.

Veronica

All this talk of love muddles my brain. I would much rather divert my
energies into my research into the Stewarts…

Diana

Charles 1 lost his head – but in a different way.

Veronica

Always remember that he did that without also losing his dignity!

*The clatter of footsteps is heard along with the voices of
Adam and Rowse in a heated conversation. They burst into the room – Rowse
supports himself with a walking stick.*

Scene 4:

Adam

He had no right to make that assumption about me –
or about my politics.

Rowse

Calm down, Adam. Hello ladies, sorry for the delay the
trains were bloody to say the least.

Adam

I do not feel like being calm, Rowse. I am insulted
and exasperated…

Veronica

What on earth is the matter?

Adam

A complete stranger on the train abused me and called me a Nazi! Just because I am German. He told me to get back to my own country as I wasn't wanted here.

Diana

Oh, dear! Don't take much notice – probably one of the green ink brigade that complains about everything. I am sure most people would never…

Adam

Sadly, that is also not true. Even your Foreign Office officials refuse to accept that not all Germans think as Hitler does. I am, it seems, not to be trusted.

Rowse

Come on now, Adam, that is taking it a bit far. For the moment Hitler is no threat to us and they have to work with him especially now it seems that he has become Chancellor.

Veronica

No! When did this happen?

Rowse

A friend at the FO gave me the nod that it will be reported on the BBC 6 O'clock news.

Adam

Why can nobody see that this is a disaster for us all?

Adam slumps into the armchair and Diana crosses to comfort him. There is an awkward moment where Rowse realizes that their relationship is more than friendly. Veronica sees the awkwardness of the situation and speaks to Rowse.

Veronica

How are you? Still using the stick?

Rowse

Better. The operation was a success to remove my duodenal ulcers but the recovery has been slow – the walking stick helps at the moment but its not permanent.

Veronica

Perhaps you need to avoid stressful situations for a while…

Rowse

At least I am not dying – I was convinced I had cancer.

Adam

I told you, Rowse, you cannot die because you have not yet lived enough!

Diana

What are you going to do, Adam? If Hitler is Chancellor as they say, where does that leave you?

Adam

I will go back home – it is still my country and I have to make the world see that not all Germans follow Hitler or his thugs.

Rowse

Maybe you could better do that by remaining here?

Veronica

Lead a resistance organization – I am sure the FO would consider that if Hitler became hostile and threatened peace.

Rowse

That is assuming that Hitler wants trouble – it is all assumptions at the moment. Perhaps he just want a better...

Adam

Nothing Hitler intends to do will make anything better for anyone – you mark my words. I feel I am living in a world where I can see the catastrophe that will unfold but nobody else can.

Veronica

What time is it?

Rowse

Just a minute to six

He crosses to the radio and switches it on. They all sit and listen expectantly apart from Adam who stands looking from the window. We hear the six o'clock time pips – this coincides with the All Souls clock chimes

BBC News Announcer

This is the BBC from London. The German government has announced today that Herr Hitler has been made the Chancellor of Germany. His National Socialist Party now has the largest number of elected members of the Reichstag. There are cheers and celebrations in Berlin, where tonight a torchlight rally is planned to celebrate this momentous victory for the Nazi Party. Downing Street said that the

Prime Minister looks forward to working with Herr Hitler for the benefit of both our countries. In other news…

Adam switches off the radio and they all sit in stunned silence for a few moments.

Diana

So it is true then…

Veronica

I feel we shall always remember this day and this time…

Adam

There will be no more elections in Germany.
Hitler is unstoppable now. Fools. Utter fools!

Rowse

In a strange way I feel somewhat relieved. At least we know what we are up against now. There is certainty in that.

Adam

I must go home of course…

Rowse

Don't do anything rash, Adam. You have your final exams in a week or so. Best not to mess that up.

Adam

I shall complete my exams – but instead of going straight to the United States for my final year I shall do a detour and go home to make sure my family are safe.

Diana

Will you have to join the Nazi party now?

Adam

Not unless I have to..

Veronica

I fear we are entering a world where we shall all be labeled or categorized for political and administrative purposes.

Diana

That sounds so cold and calculating…

Rowse

Will there be a final solution to all this?

Adam

One where I am branded as a Nazi just because I am German…

Rowse

You are Prussian, Adam!
Don't you ever forget that.

Adam crosses to Rowse and puts his arms around him and holds him. Taken aback, Rowse at first feels awkward but relaxes after a moment. Diana this time feels awkward and not pleased that Adam went to Rowse in this moment.

Veronica

I know this is probably the last thing on anyone's mind but
we have white tie ball to attend. Come along Diana, I will walk you
home to your cousin's house.

Diana

Yes, of course.

Veronica indicates they should leave.

Veronica

We will see you later on then. Dinner at eight, of course.

Veronica and Diana leave. Adam clings to Rowse. They say nothing.

The lights slowly fade to blackout.

Scene 5 :

*We see Jackers crossing the quad of All Souls on his night patrol. He holds his
lantern up and peers out front. Then exits.*

Dream & Dance Sequence

*We hear the ranting oratory of Hitler and the sounds of his triumphal procession
and the crowds shouting and cheering "heil Hitler". The music of the Al Bowlly
song introduction of With My Eyes Wide Open I am Dreaming segues through
until the crowd noise subsides and ends.*
The lights come up on Al Bowlly as he sings

With My Eyes Wide Open

Adam then dances with Diana – she also wears the yellow star that identifies her as a Jew. She rubs his arm with affection and uncovers his swastika armband. He tries to rub it away in vain.

With My Eyes Wide Open

Vickers then reveals his armband that identifies him as a member of Moseley's British Facists - Vickers does a Nazi salute to Adam. Adam then sees and dances with Rowse – he is wearing a pink triangle – the identification for homosexuals. They dance on until Rowse breaks away from him.

With My Eyes Wide Open

Adam then sees Veronica – she is also wearing a pink triangle – he tries to dance with her but she refuses and backs away.

With My Eyes Wide Open

Jackers has been in the background carrying a tray of drinks. He wears a red triangle – this marks him out as a political prisoner. Vickers enters and salutes Adam again – then exits.

Adam stands alone centre stage horrified by his armband and realizing he is branded as a Nazi in spite of being someone who is opposing them. He sees Diana and attempts to remove her yellow star but fails. He again dances with her. Under the Nazis they would all end up in concentration camps.

With My Eyes Wide Open

Adam has been left alone centre stage. He falls to his knees in tears. Rowse observes from the sidelines. After a moment he walks away.

The lights slowly fade out on a weeping Adam.

With My Eyes Wide Open

The music ends. The lights slowly fade out on Al Bowlly

Blackout.

Music Q to aid scene and time change

Scene 6:

Jackers enters on his night patrol. As he crosses, Vickers also enters and they stop and stare at one another. Vickers is wearing a black shirt and also the armband of the Moseley British fascists. He quickly puts his jacket on to cover this, and hastily exits. Jacker's watches him go and shakes his head. He then carries on with his patrol and exits.

Lights cross-fade to:

All Souls – Rowse's Rooms – 1938

It is the early hours of the morning. The sitting room is illuminated by a single side light. It is eerily quiet. After a moment we hear the shuffle of feat on the stone steps leading to the door. Then a gentle knocking – it becomes more persistent instead of louder. After a few moments Rowse comes from the bedroom and looks bleary eyed at the clock – he is wrapped in his dressing gown and wears pajamas.

Jackers (off)

Are you there Mr. Rowse?

Rowse

Jackers? What an earth is going on at
this hour of the night…

Jackers (off)

I am sorry, sir. Please open the door it's very important.

Rowse unlocks the door and opens it cautiously

Rowse

You will have the whole college awake, Jackers.

Jackers

I do hope not, sir. Forgive me, Mr. Rowse but there is someone to see you and I was unable to let him enter the college when he came this afternoon. I suggested he came back at this hour – it was the only way I could get him in to see you.

Rowse

What? Sorry, Jackers but I feel a little bemused. Let who in?

Adam

Its me, Rowse. Adam…

Rowse

Good heavens! When did you arrive in England?

Jackers

Can I ask that you gentlemen be quiet please – if anyone finds out I have let Herr Trott into the college I will be in big trouble.

Adam

Thank you, Jackers. I do appreciate your help. Here, take this…

Adam gets money from his pocket

Jackers

Oh no, sir. That will not be necessary!

Rowse

Sorry, Jackers, but what do you mean you will get
into trouble. Why?

Jackers

We were given strict instructions by the Warden not to allow Herr
Trott access if he came here. On account of him being a...

Adam

It is alright, Jackers, you can say it. Nazi!

Jackers

I am sorry, sir. I believe you when you say you are not but
others are less enlightened.

Rowse

Thank you, we will be okay now.

Jackers

I will come back for you in an hour. I must get you out before any
other college staff or Fellows wake.

*The college clock chimes 3am – it stops conversation. Jackers exits and gently
closes the door behind himself. Adam crosses to Rowse and embraces him –
Rowse doesn't react. It is only now that Rowse notices that Adam seems a little
unkempt and tired.*

Adam

I wanted to come and see you – and to see Oxford and my friends here. But it seems they do not want to see me.

Rowse

Why are you surprised? After reports of your position in the German Foreign Office, and your ill-advised letters to the Manchester Guardian newspaper defending the Nazis – little wonder that most consider you one of them.

Adam

And you? Do you believe I am one of them?

Rowse

I am not sure what to believe anymore.

Adam

I am not a spy or a double agent – nor do I want to be. That seems to be the thinking of your Foreign Office. I tried so hard to make them understand I am only part of the Nazi machine because that is where I feel I can fight it most effectively.

Rowse

Is that why you sent letters to the Guardian defending them on their treatment of the Jews – or according to you there is no mistreatment of them or anyone else. We both know that persecution and discrimination exists.

Adam

I just spoke the truth, as I experienced it as a judge in the courts. In my court we do not discriminate – or we didn't.

Rowse

So you do now? Is that what you are saying? You have to understand how this changes everything. God knows where it will end – and what consequences will be wrought onto an unsuspecting world.

Adam

I came because I wanted to see you – to see you and to say goodbye. Hitler's war is inevitable and it will come sooner than you think. I will fight this monstrous evil but I shall not survive.

Rowse

Why?

Adam

I know that I will never destroy this terrible regime. But, for future generations, I will ensure that those of us who oppose Hitler will be seen to have fought for the honour of the real Germany.

Rowse

I once said to you that you lacked the arrogance of some. I was right in that assessment of you. Your ego is unmanageable as always, but it has a halo of sincerity that is commendable. I don't flatter myself that I was anything but one of many of your admirers, but perhaps I have the edge on the others because it is your soul and intellect that I loved above anything.

Adam

That meeting of our souls is unique for me too, Rowse.

Rowse

Be careful, it would seem that Hitler despises and destroys anything and anyone that does not agree with him or fit into his category of pure and normal.

Adam

I am to be married. She is a lovely girl, much younger than me, but she will make me very happy I know. I want to make sure my children, if I am blessed to have any, will have a different life to this.

Rowse

I am glad. A good German girl? Your heritage and lineage deserves a chance. The world needs the Prussian temperament, persistence and resolve. I admire your courage above anything. It is always something I have lacked.

Adam

That is not true. I don't know anyone more courageous than you. It seems odd for me to be skulking about in the dead of night in this beautiful city.
Part of me will always remain here.
Always. Look for me in the shadows…

Rowse

Can I get you anything? A drink perhaps – I have some brandy somewhere..

Rowse gets the brandy and pours two glasses.

Adam

You don't drink – you need to watch your stomach…

Rowse

Oh that is all healed now. The best thing I ever did
having those operations. I am not afraid I am going to die anymore.

Adam

Funny, how our roles have reversed..

Rowse

I thought I could change the world but the more I see and experience
politics and politicians I realize how futile it is. Nothing is certain
anymore – even Vickers turned out to support Moseley and the
British Facists!

Adam

Some people seek the security of what they perceive is the winning
side. (*he takes a drink*) I am sorry you lost again in thirty five – but you
did come second as opposed to third in thirty one!

Rowse

Don't! Being second-rate as opposed to third-rate is nothing to be
cheery about. There is another General Election due in a few months
but I suspect it wont happen – at least that is what the constituency
secretary tells me. Looks like it will be a coalition again if war is
declared.

Adam

When. When war is declared.

They are silent for a moment and drink their brandy.

Rowse

We don't have long before Jackers comes to collect you.

Adam

I am going straight back to Germany. The Foreign Office will not
give me and my friends any help. So we will fight Hitler alone.
Remember I told you this. You are my witness for the history you
and I love so much. To be...

Rowse

[6]Or not to be [a fool and sacrifice yourself] that is the question:
Whether 'tis nobler in the mind to suffer
The slings and arrows of outrageous fortune
Or to take arms against a sea of troubles
And by opposing end them. To die, to sleep
No more and by a sleep to say we end
The heartache, and the thousand natural shocks
That flesh is heir to. 'Tis a consummation
Devoutly to be wished. To die, to sleep
To sleep perchance to dream: ay, there's the rub,

Adam

For in that sleep of death what dreams may come
When we have shuffled off this mortal coil,
Must give us pause. There's the respect
That makes calamity of so long life.
For who would bear the whips and scorns of time,
Th' opressor's wrong, the proud man's contumely
The pangs of despised love, the law's delay,
The insolence of office, and the spurns
That patient merit of th' unworthy takes,
When he himself might his quietus make
With a bare bodkin? Who would fardels bear,
To grunt and sweat under a weary life...

Rowse

But that the dread of something after death,
The undiscovered country, from whose bourn
No traveler returns, puzzles the will,
And makes us rather bear those ills we have
Than fly to others that we know not of?
Thus conscience does makes cowards of us all,
And thus the native hue of resolution
Is sicklied o'er with the pale cast of thought,
And enterprise of great pitch and moment
With this regard their currents turn awry
And lose the name of action. Soft you now,
The fair Ophelia! Nymph, in thy orisons…

Adam

…Be all my sins remembered.' Hamlet. I remember when we first
met and you recited a Shakespeare sonnet. I was captivated and have
read many of his poems and plays. That is my favourite.
Poor, foolish Hamlet.

Rowse

I plan a book on Shakespeare's sonnets and who he actually wrote
them for. In times of madness he is able to put things into a greater
perspective. He whips the cloaks from the dark ladies of history –
and reveals the secrets of human nature for us. Be they Kings,
Queens for commoners he sees through them all in spite of their
convolutions.

They sit and embrace on the sofa.
All is quiet except for the clock chiming the three quarter hour.

The lights slowly fade to blackout.

Scene: 7

The sound of an air raid siren is heard intermingled with Hitler's ranting oratory, exploding bombs and the Prime Minister Chamberlain's address to the nation on the radio that we are at war with Germany

Chamberlain [radio]

[7]'This morning the British Ambassador in Berlin handed the German Government a final note stating that, unless we heard from them by 11 o'clock that they were prepared at once to withdraw their troops from Poland, a state of war would exist between us. I have to tell you now that no such undertaking was received, and that consequently this country is at war with Germany…Now may God bless you all. May he defend the right. It is the evil things that we shall be fighting against – brute force, bad faith, injustice, oppression and persecution – and against them I am certain that right will prevail.'

Segue to:
Al Bowlly appears and sings Remember Me

Remember Me

The sound of an explosion brings this to an abrupt end and a snap blackout.

Jackers crosses with his lantern on night watch. He now wears a tin hat, instead of his bowler hat, and has a gas mask case over his shoulder. He exits.

Scene 8:
All Souls – Rowse's Rooms – 1944

The BBC radio news announcer continues:

The lights come up.

BBC News (voice over)

This is the BBC News. It has been reported that the perpetrators of the July 20th plot to assassinate Hitler by planting a bomb in his offices at Wolf's Lair have been executed today. They were tried and found guilty of treason in the People's Court within days of their failed attempt. Hitler survived the blast with minor injuries…

*Rowse sits on the edge of his desk by the window. He switches the radio off.
Veronica stands by the fireplace.*

Rowse

You have come to tell me to face the truth, haven't you? Well, I am telling you I do not want to know. I cannot think of it because if I do it chills me to my core. The maddest thing is we were all wrong, weren't we? Not that it matters but I say 'we', because even I doubted him. Even I did that!

Veronica

There are those in Oxford with a greater reason to question their conscience than you, Rowse. Please don't torture yourself.

Rowse

Why shouldn't I? Any torture I may inflict on myself is as nothing, nothing to what…to what happened to…

Veronica

Shall we have a brandy? Do you have some hidden away?

*She goes to his wall cupboard and finds a bottle and some glasses and
proceeds to pour two large glasses.*

Rowse

Such is my guilt I cannot even say his name. I do not even have the guts to allow my brain to process the spiteful and hateful sentence they carried out.

Veronica

If only the bomb had killed Hitler. [*she hands him his drink*] They say the devil looks after his own. If it had killed him, we would have been having a different conversation today.

Rowse

The worse thing is [*he swigs from his brandy*] nobody took him seriously did they. None of the buggers at the Foreign Office would give him the time of day. But in spite of that he had the courage of the abandoned and did what he could anyway. And what he did was for the honour of Germany – not his own.

Veronica

I think he knew that anyway – that it was futile. He once told me that his plan was to create an opposition to Hitler that would show future generations of Germans that not all of them followed the madman into the abyss. He wanted to create a resistance that would be remembered with pride – eventually.

Rowse

Pride? Fucking pride be dammed! I cannot believe that those beautiful liquid violet eyes will shine no more in life.

Veronica

We were lucky that he was part of our lives – we must take what we can from that. History will show that Adam was a good man even though he was misunderstood and reviled by some. Most importantly he will never be seen as a Nazi.

As the scene progresses the shadow of a lifeless hanged man slowly emerges

Rowse

They filmed it you know – his death. So that Hitler could sit in the luxury of his private cinema and watch those who tried to assassinate him die.

Veronica

Don't do this to yourself…

Rowse

I must. Don't you see that I must face what happened to him and we must make sure the world never forgets the barbarity of it. Piano wire.

Veronica

The best we can hope for is that it was quick…

Rowse

But Veronica, don't you see, the whole point was to make sure that he and his friends suffered the worst possible death.

Veronica

How do we know for sure anyway…

Rowse

The Nazis delighted in broadcasting the details – to exert as much fear as possible on anyone who had ideas to usurp Hitler and his mob. An old student at the FO found out for me.

Veronica

What about Adam's wife and children? Where are they?

Rowse

Nobody knows they have been interred along with other members of his family. Taken away in the night.

Veronica

His two daughters are only toddlers – surely they will not be harmed?

Rowse

They used piano wire.

The shadow of the hanged man is now definite and defined. It is Adam's lifeless body. The shadow casts itself across the scene.

Veronica

Why?

Rowse

To inflict the cruelest and most painful of deaths. Slowly the wire tightens with the weight of the body and chokes the life away. The wire slowly starts to cut into the flesh of the neck, like a slow beheading as it slices deeper and deeper. Then it works on the spinal cord. There is no way to cry out or scream. The screams only in the heads of those being slowly decapitated.

Veronica

Stop it, Rowse. Please stop it! What good is this. All you are doing is disturbing your mind. I want to remember Adam as the young, vibrant and intelligent man we knew. He was always different and seemed to have an idea of his destiny as I recall.

Rowse

We had this mad idea that we could change the world. That through politics we could make the world a better place, a more equal place. Walk through Oxford, or any town or city, and they are all the same.

Veronica

Who are?

Rowse

People.[8] 'I don't like other people; I particularly don't like their children; I deeply disapprove of their proliferation making the globe uninhabitable. The fucking idiots –
I don't want to pay for their fucking!'

Veronica

You can't say that! Having children is human nature,
it is how we continue.

Rowse

One day I will tell the world what I think – and care even less! It is all they care about. Why must we continue? Look at the mess this world is in now? There are horrors to be yet revealed as a result of this war. I would not want to bring a child into this world myself to suffer the consequences....

The shadows of the hanging Adam suddenly disappears as the body falls away from the head in the moment of decapitation. The wire swings hauntingly and casts its shadow over them.

Rowse

[9] 'Summer will come, and make you brave to war
And harden you…
And Autumn will lay a still, cold finger
On your beauty, and dim your liquid eyes
And suck the juices of your lips.
This living dream you are shall see eclipse
And I'll not mourn you in my waking state,
Wide-eyed and frozen of heart.

Rowse flings a book across the room in despair

[10]'This filthy twentieth century. I hate its guts!'

The lights come up on an empty microphone and stand.

BBC Radio Announcer

An now on the light programme in memory of Al Bowlly who was killed in an air raid on his London home.

We hear Al Bowlly singing Cole Porter's Night and Day :

Night & Day

*The lights slowly fade on the microphone stand.
The song ends. Blackout.*

The End

Other People's Fu**ing!

An Oxford Affair.

ABOUT THE AUTHOR

David Slattery-Christy is an award-winning playwright and author. His new novel The Mistletoe Haunting - Legend of Minster Lovell released 26 February 2016: "A beautiful book, and beautifully written." Kat Orman, BBC Radio Oxford 22/1/16 ***Author and his Novello biography 'In Search of Ruritania' Featured on BBC Radio 2 documentary on Ivor Novello with Don Black titled: Keep The Home Fires Burning as part of the BBC Great War Centenary broadcasts. *** Also featured on the BBC Radio 3 'Composer of the Week' programme dedicated to Ivor Novello.

David was born in Oxford, England, in 1959. He graduated from London's City University with a BA (Hons) Degree in Journalism. In addition to this he has a Teaching Degree from Lancaster University and a Masters Degree in the Arts from the University of Central Lancashire and continues his professional development by undertaking research and history courses at the University of Oxford. Prior to this he attended London Theatre Arts to study drama, and then worked extensively in the performing arts industry as a playwright, producer and director. His stage plays include the award winning Forever Nineteen, After The Tone and The Post Card - which enjoyed London and New York productions, as well as touring nationally in the United Kingdom. His involvement in adapting the libretto for Ivor Novello's 1935 musical Glamorous Night resulted in him directing the 50th Anniversary Concert to celebrate the life and work of Novello at the Theatre Royal, Drury Lane, in London's West End. Subsequently he has worked as the Ivor Novello Consultant on Julian Fellowes and Robert Altman's Oscar and BAFTA winning film Gosford Park, and contributed to the BBC Documentary on the life of Novello The Handsomest Man in Britain. He is the author of In Search of Ruritania, a biography on Ivor Novello - Anything But Merry! The Life and Times of Lily Elsie the Edwardian actress and singer who found fame in Lehar's The Merry Widow; the novel based on the legend of a mistletoe bride titled The Mistletoe Haunting: Legend of Minster Lovell and a WW1 biography Mildred on the Marne: Mildred Aldrich, Front-line Witness 1914-1918. Currently he is developing a play based on the relationship between opera composer Puccini and his wife, Elvira.

Further information available at: www.christyplays.com

Printed in Great Britain
by Amazon